The Magic of the Matrix

Practice Arithmetic while Having Fun

by Ian Ward

Contents

	Page
How to construct a matrix	2
3 × 3 matrices	5
4 × 4 matrices	9
5 × 5 matrices	17
6 × 6 matrices	25
7 × 7 and 8 × 8 matrices	29
9 × 9 and 10 × 10 matrices	30
3 × 3 decimal matrices	31
3 × 3 fraction matrices	33
3 × 3 decimal/fraction matrices	35
4 × 4 matrices – incomplete	37
5 × 5 matrices – incomplete	40
Multiplication matrices	41
Answers	43

How to use the Matrix

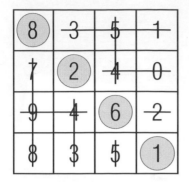 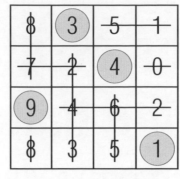 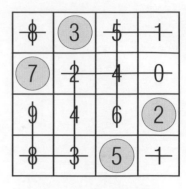

| 8 + 2 + 6 + 1 = 17 | 9 + 3 + 4 + 1 = 17 | 7 + 3 + 5 + 2 = 17 |

A single matrix can be copied for all the class or at a party and as each child selects their own numbers and totals them, all the class find that they have the same total! This can be repeated at suitable intervals throughout the whole school year if desired. The children will probably, at some stage, want to know the "secret" of the Magic Matrix, and how the teacher can predict the answer when children are selecting different numbers using the same matrix. The teacher can then choose a suitable opportunity to reveal how they are constructed (see pages iii to vi) and children can then construct their own and amaze their friends and parents!

A single page can be photocopied for all the children as either a whole class activity or for homework. There is a sufficient variety of matrices to make differentiation easy to implement. This is a simple exercise in addition at various levels, but the fact that the same matrix has been duplicated two or three times means that this is a self-checking exercise – they will always get the same answer. eg 17

N.B. What ever the size of the matrix their should be a corresponding list of numbers to add up.

Matrix

3 x 3 = 3 numbers to total

4 x 4 = 4 numbers to total

5 x 5 = 5 numbers to total

etc.

How to construct a Matrix

The Unknown Total: Method 1

In this method the Matrix Total is not known until the matrix is completed.

Step 1

Using a blank matrix complete a row with appropriate numbers.

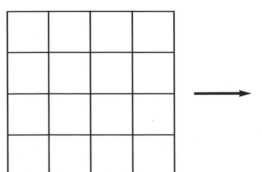 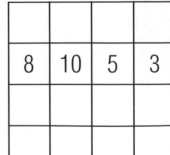

Step 2

To this completed row decide what to add or subtract to/from each number eg add 5, and complete either the row above or below.

13	15	10	8
8	10	5	3

+5

Step 3

Repeat this procedure for the row below, again selecting a number either to add or subtract from the row created in the Step 2 eg subtract 2.

Beware of constructing a matrix that results in negative numbers being displayed.

13	15	10	8
8	10	5	3
6	8	3	1

+5

−2

Step 4

Repeat for the final row eg + 7

13	15	10	8
8	10	5	3
6	8	3	1
13	15	10	8

+5

−2

+7

N.B. To find the Matrix Total without marking the grid, add the two diagonal series of numbers and they should be the same as in this example 34.

The Unknown Total: Method 2

In this method the Matrix Total is known before the matrix is completed in the example that follows.

Step 1

Using a blank matrix complete a diagonal so that the total of the numbers is 15.

5			
	3		
		4	
			3

Step 2

Select the "4" and, for example, decide to add 2 to this number. Enter the result in the square above the "4".

Conversely subtract 2 from the "3" and enter the result in the box below the "3".

5			
	3	6	
	1	4	
			3

Step 3

Complete the remaining diagonal with any numbers so that the total is 15.

5			5
	3	6	
	1	4	
3			3

Step 4

Put a number in the second square in the top row eg 6.

You may wish to go back and change this if the completed matrix results in negative numbers being displayed.

5	6		5
	3	6	
	1	4	
3			3

Step 5

We can see, from the numbers shown, that the difference between the top row and the second row is 3. Following the pattern described in Step 2 add the difference to complete the top row and the second row. The top two rows can now be completed.

The difference between the second and third rows is 2. Follow the pattern and complete the third row.

Finally the difference between the third and fourth row is 3. Complete the bottom row and the matrix is finished.

5	6	9	5
2	3	6	2
	1	4	
3			3

5	6	9	5
2	3	6	2
0	1	4	0
3			3

5	6	9	5
2	3	6	2
0	1	4	0
3	4	7	3

3 × 3 matrices

Circle any number in a row and cross out the others in that row and column. Repeat this process until there is only one number remaining and circle this final number. Add up all the circled numbers. Choose different numbers in the next matrix and add the total of the circled numbers in each. What do you find?

9	5	4
6	2	1
7	3	2

9	5	4
6	2	1
7	3	2

Matrix Total _____ (a)

5	6	7
7	8	9
4	5	6

5	6	7
7	8	9
4	5	6

Matrix Total _____ (b)

6	7	8
1	2	3
4	5	6

6	7	8
1	2	3
4	5	6

Matrix Total _____ (c)

4	3	9
2	1	7
3	2	8

4	3	9
2	1	7
3	2	8

Matrix Total _____ (d)

3	2	5
5	4	7
6	5	8

3	2	5
5	4	7
6	5	8

Matrix Total _____ (e)

7	4	3
4	1	0
5	2	1

7	4	3
4	1	0
5	2	1

Matrix Total _____ (f)

7	9	7
5	7	5
4	6	4

7	9	7
5	7	5
4	6	4

Matrix Total _____ (g)

9	9	5
5	5	1
7	7	3

9	9	5
5	5	1
7	7	3

Matrix Total _____ (h)

Circle any number in a row and cross out the others in that row and column. Repeat this process until there is only one number remaining and circle this final number. Add up all the circled numbers. Choose different numbers in the next matrix and add the total of the circled numbers in each. What do you find?

4	1	4
8	5	8
9	6	9

4	1	4
8	5	8
9	6	9

Matrix Total _____ (a)

2	2	4
5	5	7
7	7	9

2	2	4
5	5	7
7	7	9

Matrix Total _____ (b)

6	5	6
4	3	4
1	0	1

6	5	6
4	3	4
1	0	1

Matrix Total _____ (c)

8	6	8
3	1	3
5	3	5

8	6	8
3	1	3
5	3	5

Matrix Total _____ (d)

4	0	2
6	2	4
7	3	5

4	0	2
6	2	4
7	3	5

Matrix Total _____ (e)

5	8	4
2	5	1
4	7	3

5	8	4
2	5	1
4	7	3

Matrix Total _____ (f)

5	2	5
7	4	7
8	5	8

5	2	5
7	4	7
8	5	8

Matrix Total _____ (g)

9	5	6
6	2	3
4	0	1

9	5	6
6	2	3
4	0	1

Matrix Total _____ (h)

3 × 3 matrices *(continued)*

Circle any number in a row and cross out the others in that row and column. Repeat this process until there is only one number remaining and circle this final number. Add up all the circled numbers. Choose different numbers in the next matrix and add the total of the circled numbers in each. What do you find?

5	4	2
7	6	4
4	3	1

5	4	2
7	6	4
4	3	1

Matrix Total _____ (a)

7	1	4
9	3	6
8	2	5

7	1	4
9	3	6
8	2	5

Matrix Total _____ (b)

6	2	6
8	4	8
4	0	4

6	2	6
8	4	8
4	0	4

Matrix Total _____ (c)

5	4	1
8	7	4
6	5	2

5	4	1
8	7	4
6	5	2

Matrix Total _____ (d)

8	7	6
6	5	4
2	1	0

8	7	6
6	5	4
2	1	0

Matrix Total _____ (e)

6	1	0
9	4	3
7	2	1

6	1	0
9	4	3
7	2	1

Matrix Total _____ (f)

6	5	1
7	6	2
8	7	3

6	5	1
7	6	2
8	7	3

Matrix Total _____ (g)

8	3	7
5	0	4
7	2	6

8	3	7
5	0	4
7	2	6

Matrix Total _____ (h)

3 × 3 matrices *(continued)*

Circle any number in a row and cross out the others in that row and column. Repeat this process until there is only one number remaining and circle this final number. Add up all the circled numbers. Choose different numbers in the next matrix and add the total of the circled numbers in each. What do you find?

33	22	32
21	10	20
14	3	13

33	22	32
21	10	20
14	3	13

Matrix Total _____ (a)

19	27	27
16	24	24
18	26	26

19	27	27
16	24	24
18	26	26

Matrix Total _____ (b)

15	12	24
22	19	31
22	19	31

15	12	24
22	19	31
22	19	31

Matrix Total _____ (c)

17	30	20
12	25	15
15	28	18

17	30	20
12	25	15
15	28	18

Matrix Total _____ (d)

13	15	19
16	18	22
9	11	15

13	15	19
16	18	22
9	11	15

Matrix Total _____ (e)

24	18	22
20	14	18
11	5	9

24	18	22
20	14	18
11	5	9

Matrix Total _____ (f)

33	22	17
22	11	6
20	9	4

33	22	17
22	11	6
20	9	4

Matrix Total _____ (g)

11	3	7
18	10	14
12	4	8

11	3	7
18	10	14
12	4	8

Matrix Total _____ (h)

The Magic of the Matrix   © tarquin publications

4 × 4 matrices

Circle any number in a row and cross out the others in that row and column. Repeat this process until there is only one number remaining and circle this final number. Add up all the circled numbers. Choose different numbers in the next matrix and add the total of the circled numbers in each. What do you find?

5	1	0	2
8	4	3	5
9	5	4	6
6	2	1	3

5	1	0	2
8	4	3	5
9	5	4	6
6	2	1	3

5	1	0	2
8	4	3	5
9	5	4	6
6	2	1	3

Matrix Total

_____

(a)

6	4	1	3
7	5	2	4
5	3	0	2
9	7	4	6

6	4	1	3
7	5	2	4
5	3	0	2
9	7	4	6

6	4	1	3
7	5	2	4
5	3	0	2
9	7	4	6

Matrix Total

_____

(b)

6	5	6	4
7	6	7	5
2	1	2	0
4	3	4	2

6	5	6	4
7	6	7	5
2	1	2	0
4	3	4	2

6	5	6	4
7	6	7	5
2	1	2	0
4	3	4	2

Matrix Total

_____

(c)

8	3	5	1
7	2	4	0
9	4	6	2
8	3	5	1

8	3	5	1
7	2	4	0
9	4	6	2
8	3	5	1

8	3	5	1
7	2	4	0
9	4	6	2
8	3	5	1

Matrix Total

_____

(d)

4 × 4 matrices (continued)

Circle any number in a row and cross out the others in that row and column. Repeat this process until there is only one number remaining and circle this final number. Add up all the circled numbers. Choose different numbers in the next matrix and add the total of the circled numbers in each. What do you find?

7	8	6	3
8	9	7	4
6	7	5	2
4	5	3	0

7	8	6	3
8	9	7	4
6	7	5	2
4	5	3	0

7	8	6	3
8	9	7	4
6	7	5	2
4	5	3	0

Matrix Total

_____

(a)

2	5	4	7
4	7	6	9
1	4	3	6
3	6	5	8

2	5	4	7
4	7	6	9
1	4	3	6
3	6	5	8

2	5	4	7
4	7	6	9
1	4	3	6
3	6	5	8

Matrix Total

_____

(b)

1	1	3	0
5	5	7	4
7	7	9	6
6	6	8	5

1	1	3	0
5	5	7	4
7	7	9	6
6	6	8	5

1	1	3	0
5	5	7	4
7	7	9	6
6	6	8	5

Matrix Total

_____

(c)

1	0	2	0
3	2	4	2
7	6	8	6
6	5	7	5

1	0	2	0
3	2	4	2
7	6	8	6
6	5	7	5

1	0	2	0
3	2	4	2
7	6	8	6
6	5	7	5

Matrix Total

_____

(d)

4 × 4 matrices *(continued)*

Circle any number in a row and cross out the others in that row and column. Repeat this process until there is only one number remaining and circle this final number. Add up all the circled numbers. Choose different numbers in the next matrix and add the total of the circled numbers in each. What do you find?

6	5	5	3
4	3	3	1
9	8	8	6
7	6	6	4

6	5	5	3
4	3	3	1
9	8	8	6
7	6	6	4

6	5	5	3
4	3	3	1
9	8	8	6
7	6	6	4

Matrix Total

_____

(a)

5	1	5	8
6	2	6	9
4	0	4	7
5	1	5	8

5	1	5	8
6	2	6	9
4	0	4	7
5	1	5	8

5	1	5	8
6	2	6	9
4	0	4	7
5	1	5	8

Matrix Total

_____

(b)

3	5	5	1
5	7	7	3
7	9	9	5
6	8	8	4

3	5	5	1
5	7	7	3
7	9	9	5
6	8	8	4

3	5	5	1
5	7	7	3
7	9	9	5
6	8	8	4

Matrix Total

_____

(c)

6	3	8	4
4	1	6	2
7	4	9	5
5	2	7	3

6	3	8	4
4	1	6	2
7	4	9	5
5	2	7	3

6	3	8	4
4	1	6	2
7	4	9	5
5	2	7	3

Matrix Total

_____

(d)

4 × 4 matrices (continued)

Circle any number in a row and cross out the others in that row and column. Repeat this process until there is only one number remaining and circle this final number. Add up all the circled numbers. Choose different numbers in the next matrix and add the total of the circled numbers in each. What do you find?

4	2	0	1
6	4	2	3
8	6	4	5
9	7	5	6

4	2	0	1
6	4	2	3
8	6	4	5
9	7	5	6

4	2	0	1
6	4	2	3
8	6	4	5
9	7	5	6

Matrix Total

_____

(a)

9	7	8	9
7	5	6	7
5	3	4	5
4	2	3	4

9	7	8	9
7	5	6	7
5	3	4	5
4	2	3	4

9	7	8	9
7	5	6	7
5	3	4	5
4	2	3	4

Matrix Total

_____

(b)

6	6	3	4
9	9	6	7
7	7	4	5
3	3	0	1

6	6	3	4
9	9	6	7
7	7	4	5
3	3	0	1

6	6	3	4
9	9	6	7
7	7	4	5
3	3	0	1

Matrix Total

_____

(c)

9	6	2	5
7	4	0	3
9	6	2	5
8	5	1	4

9	6	2	5
7	4	0	3
9	6	2	5
8	5	1	4

9	6	2	5
7	4	0	3
9	6	2	5
8	5	1	4

Matrix Total

_____

(d)

4 × 4 matrices *(continued)*

Circle any number in a row and cross out the others in that row and column. Repeat this process until there is only one number remaining and circle this final number. Add up all the circled numbers. Choose different numbers in the next matrix and add the total of the circled numbers in each. What do you find?

3	3	1	0
6	6	4	3
8	8	6	5
5	5	3	2

3	3	1	0
6	6	4	3
8	8	6	5
5	5	3	2

3	3	1	0
6	6	4	3
8	8	6	5
5	5	3	2

Matrix Total

——————

(a)

3	6	4	5
4	7	5	6
6	9	7	8
3	6	4	5

3	6	4	5
4	7	5	6
6	9	7	8
3	6	4	5

3	6	4	5
4	7	5	6
6	9	7	8
3	6	4	5

Matrix Total

——————

(b)

8	7	8	9
4	3	4	5
5	4	5	6
2	1	2	3

8	7	8	9
4	3	4	5
5	4	5	6
2	1	2	3

8	7	8	9
4	3	4	5
5	4	5	6
2	1	2	3

Matrix Total

——————

(c)

6	8	6	4
5	7	5	3
7	9	7	5
2	4	2	0

6	8	6	4
5	7	5	3
7	9	7	5
2	4	2	0

6	8	6	4
5	7	5	3
7	9	7	5
2	4	2	0

Matrix Total

——————

(d)

4 × 4 matrices *(continued)*

Circle any number in a row and cross out the others in that row and column. Repeat this process until there is only one number remaining and circle this final number. Add up all the circled numbers. Choose different numbers in the next matrix and add the total of the circled numbers in each. What do you find?

6	4	0	2
8	6	2	4
9	7	3	5
7	5	1	3

6	4	0	2
8	6	2	4
9	7	3	5
7	5	1	3

6	4	0	2
8	6	2	4
9	7	3	5
7	5	1	3

Matrix Total

_____

(a)

5	0	3	2
9	4	7	6
6	1	4	3
8	3	6	5

5	0	3	2
9	4	7	6
6	1	4	3
8	3	6	5

5	0	3	2
9	4	7	6
6	1	4	3
8	3	6	5

Matrix Total

_____

(b)

3	1	4	2
6	4	7	5
8	6	9	7
4	2	5	3

3	1	4	2
6	4	7	5
8	6	9	7
4	2	5	3

3	1	4	2
6	4	7	5
8	6	9	7
4	2	5	3

Matrix Total

_____

(c)

4	4	1	1
7	7	4	4
9	9	6	6
6	6	3	3

4	4	1	1
7	7	4	4
9	9	6	6
6	6	3	3

4	4	1	1
7	7	4	4
9	9	6	6
6	6	3	3

Matrix Total

_____

(d)

4 × 4 matrices *(continued)*

Circle any number in a row and cross out the others in that row and column. Repeat this process until there is only one number remaining and circle this final number. Add up all the circled numbers. Choose different numbers in the next matrix and add the total of the circled numbers in each. What do you find?

11	18	11	12
15	22	15	16
21	28	21	22
12	19	12	13

11	18	11	12
15	22	15	16
21	28	21	22
12	19	12	13

11	18	11	12
15	22	15	16
21	28	21	22
12	19	12	13

Matrix Total

_____

(a)

19	23	11	10
17	21	9	8
14	18	6	5
30	34	22	21

19	23	11	10
17	21	9	8
14	18	6	5
30	34	22	21

19	23	11	10
17	21	9	8
14	18	6	5
30	34	22	21

Matrix Total

_____

(b)

16	10	25	17
14	8	23	15
24	18	33	25
10	4	19	11

16	10	25	17
14	8	23	15
24	18	33	25
10	4	19	11

16	10	25	17
14	8	23	15
24	18	33	25
10	4	19	11

Matrix Total

_____

(c)

23	11	14	24
28	16	19	29
17	5	8	18
32	20	23	33

23	11	14	24
28	16	19	29
17	5	8	18
32	20	23	33

23	11	14	24
28	16	19	29
17	5	8	18
32	20	23	33

Matrix Total

_____

(d)

4 × 4 matrices (continued)

Circle any number in a row and cross out the others in that row and column. Repeat this process until there is only one number remaining and circle this final number. Add up all the circled numbers. Choose different numbers in the next matrix and add the total of the circled numbers in each. What do you find?

7	19	20	20
24	36	37	37
12	24	25	25
15	27	28	28

7	19	20	20
24	36	37	37
12	24	25	25
15	27	28	28

7	19	20	20
24	36	37	37
12	24	25	25
15	27	28	28

Matrix Total

_____

(a)

16	22	20	19
20	26	24	23
21	27	25	24
11	17	15	14

16	22	20	19
20	26	24	23
21	27	25	24
11	17	15	14

16	22	20	19
20	26	24	23
21	27	25	24
11	17	15	14

Matrix Total

_____

(b)

32	31	16	33
24	23	8	25
28	27	12	29
21	20	5	22

32	31	16	33
24	23	8	25
28	27	12	29
21	20	5	22

32	31	16	33
24	23	8	25
28	27	12	29
21	20	5	22

Matrix Total

_____

(c)

28	20	25	22
38	30	35	32
18	10	15	12
22	14	19	16

28	20	25	22
38	30	35	32
18	10	15	12
22	14	19	16

28	20	25	22
38	30	35	32
18	10	15	12
22	14	19	16

Matrix Total

_____

(d)

The Magic of the Matrix

5 × 5 matrices

Circle any number in a row and cross out the others in that row and column. Repeat this process until there is only one number remaining and circle this final number. Add up all the circled numbers. Choose different numbers in the next matrix and add the total of the circled numbers in each. What do you find?

4	6	8	10	7
6	8	10	12	9
1	3	5	7	4
3	5	7	9	6
0	2	4	6	3

4	6	8	10	7
6	8	10	12	9
1	3	5	7	4
3	5	7	9	6
0	2	4	6	3

Matrix Total _____ (a)

5	9	6	7	12
4	8	5	6	11
0	4	1	2	7
3	7	4	5	10
2	6	3	4	9

5	9	6	7	12
4	8	5	6	11
0	4	1	2	7
3	7	4	5	10
2	6	3	4	9

Matrix Total _____ (b)

5	5	7	4	3
7	7	9	6	5
2	2	4	1	0
3	3	5	2	1
6	6	8	5	4

5	5	7	4	3
7	7	9	6	5
2	2	4	1	0
3	3	5	2	1
6	6	8	5	4

Matrix Total _____ (c)

Circle any number in a row and cross out the others in that row and column. Repeat this process until there is only one number remaining and circle this final number. Add up all the circled numbers. Choose different numbers in the next matrix and add the total of the circled numbers in each. What do you find?

6	5	8	9	7
7	6	9	10	8
1	0	3	4	2
4	3	6	7	5
3	2	5	6	4

6	5	8	9	7
7	6	9	10	8
1	0	3	4	2
4	3	6	7	5
3	2	5	6	4

Matrix Total _____ (a)

5	5	7	3	4
7	7	9	5	6
4	4	6	2	3
2	2	4	0	1
6	6	8	4	5

5	5	7	3	4
7	7	9	5	6
4	4	6	2	3
2	2	4	0	1
6	6	8	4	5

Matrix Total _____ (b)

9	3	6	8	4
10	4	7	9	5
7	1	4	6	2
8	2	5	7	3
6	0	3	5	1

9	3	6	8	4
10	4	7	9	5
7	1	4	6	2
8	2	5	7	3
6	0	3	5	1

Matrix Total _____ (c)

5 × 5 matrices (continued)

Circle any number in a row and cross out the others in that row and column. Repeat this process until there is only one number remaining and circle this final number. Add up all the circled numbers. Choose different numbers in the next matrix and add the total of the circled numbers in each. What do you find?

7	1	3	3	5
10	4	6	6	8
9	3	5	5	7
6	0	2	2	4
8	2	4	4	6

7	1	3	3	5
10	4	6	6	8
9	3	5	5	7
6	0	2	2	4
8	2	4	4	6

Matrix Total _____ (a)

5	2	5	6	4
8	5	8	9	7
7	4	7	8	6
3	0	3	4	2
4	1	4	5	3

5	2	5	6	4
8	5	8	9	7
7	4	7	8	6
3	0	3	4	2
4	1	4	5	3

Matrix Total _____ (b)

6	0	5	6	1
11	5	10	11	6
8	2	7	8	3
7	1	6	7	2
10	4	9	10	5

6	0	5	6	1
11	5	10	11	6
8	2	7	8	3
7	1	6	7	2
10	4	9	10	5

Matrix Total _____ (c)

5 × 5 matrices *(continued)*

Circle any number in a row and cross out the others in that row and column. Repeat this process until there is only one number remaining and circle this final number. Add up all the circled numbers. Choose different numbers in the next matrix and add the total of the circled numbers in each. What do you find?

5	3	4	8	5
4	2	3	7	4
3	1	2	6	3
8	6	7	11	8
7	5	6	10	7

5	3	4	8	5
4	2	3	7	4
3	1	2	6	3
8	6	7	11	8
7	5	6	10	7

Matrix Total _____ (a)

2	3	4	5	0
5	6	7	8	3
6	7	8	9	4
3	4	5	6	1
7	8	9	10	5

2	3	4	5	0
5	6	7	8	3
6	7	8	9	4
3	4	5	6	1
7	8	9	10	5

Matrix Total _____ (b)

5	4	3	3	6
2	1	0	0	3
7	6	5	5	8
6	5	4	4	7
4	3	2	2	5

5	4	3	3	6
2	1	0	0	3
7	6	5	5	8
6	5	4	4	7
4	3	2	2	5

Matrix Total _____ (c)

5 × 5 matrices (continued)

Circle any number in a row and cross out the others in that row and column. Repeat this process until there is only one number remaining and circle this final number. Add up all the circled numbers. Choose different numbers in the next matrix and add the total of the circled numbers in each. What do you find?

8	3	4	5	5
7	2	3	4	4
9	4	5	6	6
8	3	4	5	5
5	0	1	2	2

8	3	4	5	5
7	2	3	4	4
9	4	5	6	6
8	3	4	5	5
5	0	1	2	2

Matrix Total _____ (a)

7	2	4	3	1
10	5	7	6	4
6	1	3	2	0
8	3	5	4	2
9	4	6	5	3

7	2	4	3	1
10	5	7	6	4
6	1	3	2	0
8	3	5	4	2
9	4	6	5	3

Matrix Total _____ (b)

6	7	8	4	3
8	9	10	6	5
5	6	7	3	2
3	4	5	1	0
7	8	9	5	4

6	7	8	4	3
8	9	10	6	5
5	6	7	3	2
3	4	5	1	0
7	8	9	5	4

Matrix Total _____ (c)

The Magic of the Matrix

5 × 5 matrices (continued)

Circle any number in a row and cross out the others in that row and column. Repeat this process until there is only one number remaining and circle this final number. Add up all the circled numbers. Choose different numbers in the next matrix and add the total of the circled numbers in each. What do you find?

7	7	3	5	1
14	14	10	12	8
9	9	5	7	3
6	6	2	4	0
8	8	4	6	2

7	7	3	5	1
14	14	10	12	8
9	9	5	7	3
6	6	2	4	0
8	8	4	6	2

Matrix Total _____ (a)

10	8	7	11	5
5	3	2	6	0
8	6	5	9	3
6	4	3	7	1
7	5	4	8	2

10	8	7	11	5
5	3	2	6	0
8	6	5	9	3
6	4	3	7	1
7	5	4	8	2

Matrix Total _____ (b)

4	4	2	1	5
5	5	3	2	6
7	7	5	4	8
6	6	4	3	7
11	11	9	8	12

4	4	2	1	5
5	5	3	2	6
7	7	5	4	8
6	6	4	3	7
11	11	9	8	12

Matrix Total _____ (c)

5 × 5 matrices (continued)

Circle any number in a row and cross out the others in that row and column. Repeat this process until there is only one number remaining and circle this final number. Add up all the circled numbers. Choose different numbers in the next matrix and add the total of the circled numbers in each. What do you find?

8	5	4	7	5
7	4	3	6	4
4	1	0	3	1
9	6	5	8	6
6	3	2	5	3

8	5	4	7	5
7	4	3	6	4
4	1	0	3	1
9	6	5	8	6
6	3	2	5	3

Matrix Total _____ (a)

6	8	4	5	4
7	9	5	6	5
4	6	2	3	2
9	11	7	8	7
8	10	6	7	6

6	8	4	5	4
7	9	5	6	5
4	6	2	3	2
9	11	7	8	7
8	10	6	7	6

Matrix Total _____ (b)

6	6	3	2	7
9	9	6	5	10
5	5	2	1	6
8	8	5	4	9
7	7	4	3	8

6	6	3	2	7
9	9	6	5	10
5	5	2	1	6
8	8	5	4	9
7	7	4	3	8

Matrix Total _____ (c)

Circle any number in a row and cross out the others in that row and column. Repeat this process until there is only one number remaining and circle this final number. Add up all the circled numbers. Choose different numbers in the next matrix and add the total of the circled numbers in each. What do you find?

2	0	1	6	3
7	5	6	11	8
6	4	5	10	7
3	1	2	7	4
4	2	3	8	5

2	0	1	6	3
7	5	6	11	8
6	4	5	10	7
3	1	2	7	4
4	2	3	8	5

Matrix Total _____ (a)

13	6	8	5	9
12	5	7	4	8
8	1	3	0	4
10	3	5	2	6
11	4	6	3	7

13	6	8	5	9
12	5	7	4	8
8	1	3	0	4
10	3	5	2	6
11	4	6	3	7

Matrix Total _____ (b)

5	4	5	6	9
1	0	1	2	5
3	2	3	4	7
7	6	7	8	11
6	5	6	7	10

5	4	5	6	9
1	0	1	2	5
3	2	3	4	7
7	6	7	8	11
6	5	6	7	10

Matrix Total _____ (c)

6 × 6 matrices

Circle any number in a row and cross out the others in that row and column. Repeat this process until there is only one number remaining and circle this final number. Add up all the circled numbers. Choose different numbers in the next matrix and add the total of the circled numbers in each. What do you find?

8	4	6	8	5	2
7	3	5	7	4	1
9	5	7	9	6	3
6	2	4	6	3	0
8	4	6	8	5	2
7	3	5	7	4	1

Matrix Total

_____

(a)

8	4	6	8	5	2
7	3	5	7	4	1
9	5	7	9	6	3
6	2	4	6	3	0
8	4	6	8	5	2
7	3	5	7	4	1

3	1	3	0	5	4
5	3	5	2	7	6
7	5	7	4	9	8
4	2	4	1	6	5
6	4	6	3	8	7
3	1	3	0	5	4

Matrix Total

_____

(b)

3	1	3	0	5	4
5	3	5	2	7	6
7	5	7	4	9	8
4	2	4	1	6	5
6	4	6	3	8	7
3	1	3	0	5	4

4	4	1	2	2	5
6	6	3	4	4	7
7	7	4	5	5	8
5	5	2	3	3	6
8	8	5	6	6	9
3	3	0	1	1	4

Matrix Total

_____

(c)

4	4	1	2	2	5
6	6	3	4	4	7
7	7	4	5	5	8
5	5	2	3	3	6
8	8	5	6	6	9
3	3	0	1	1	4

6 × 6 matrices *(continued)*

Circle any number in a row and cross out the others in that row and column. Repeat this process until there is only one number remaining and circle this final number. Add up all the circled numbers. Choose different numbers in the next matrix and add the total of the circled numbers in each. What do you find?

7	5	3	6	4	6
8	6	4	7	5	7
5	3	1	4	2	4
4	2	0	3	1	3
6	4	2	5	3	5
9	7	5	8	6	8

Matrix Total

—————————

(a)

7	5	3	6	4	6
8	6	4	7	5	7
5	3	1	4	2	4
4	2	0	3	1	3
6	4	2	5	3	5
9	7	5	8	6	8

5	2	1	1	3	5
6	3	2	2	4	6
7	4	3	3	5	7
9	6	5	5	7	9
8	5	4	4	6	8
4	1	0	0	2	4

Matrix Total

—————————

(b)

5	2	1	1	3	5
6	3	2	2	4	6
7	4	3	3	5	7
9	6	5	5	7	9
8	5	4	4	6	8
4	1	0	0	2	4

8	7	8	6	9	5
7	6	7	5	8	4
5	4	5	3	6	2
3	2	3	1	4	0
8	7	8	6	9	5
4	3	4	2	5	1

Matrix Total

—————————

(c)

8	7	8	6	9	5
7	6	7	5	8	4
5	4	5	3	6	2
3	2	3	1	4	0
8	7	8	6	9	5
4	3	4	2	5	1

6 × 6 matrices *(continued)*

Circle any number in a row and cross out the others in that row and column. Repeat this process until there is only one number remaining and circle this final number. Add up all the circled numbers. Choose different numbers in the next matrix and add the total of the circled numbers in each. What do you find?

5	2	3	2	4	1
8	5	6	5	7	4
6	3	4	3	5	2
9	6	7	6	8	5
7	4	5	4	6	3
4	1	2	1	3	0

Matrix Total

_____

(a)

5	2	3	2	4	1
8	5	6	5	7	4
6	3	4	3	5	2
9	6	7	6	8	5
7	4	5	4	6	3
4	1	2	1	3	0

4	1	0	0	3	2
5	2	1	1	4	3
7	4	3	3	6	5
9	6	5	5	8	7
6	3	2	2	5	4
8	5	4	4	7	6

Matrix Total

_____

(b)

4	1	0	0	3	2
5	2	1	1	4	3
7	4	3	3	6	5
9	6	5	5	8	7
6	3	2	2	5	4
8	5	4	4	7	6

6	3	4	1	5	4
7	4	5	2	6	5
5	2	3	0	4	3
8	5	6	3	7	6
6	3	4	1	5	4
7	4	5	2	6	5

Matrix Total

_____

(c)

6	3	4	1	5	4
7	4	5	2	6	5
5	2	3	0	4	3
8	5	6	3	7	6
6	3	4	1	5	4
7	4	5	2	6	5

6 × 6 matrices *(continued)*

Circle any number in a row and cross out the others in that row and column. Repeat this process until there is only one number remaining and circle this final number. Add up all the circled numbers. Choose different numbers in the next matrix and add the total of the circled numbers in each. What do you find?

6	4	4	3	7	6
5	3	3	2	6	5
8	6	6	5	9	8
4	2	2	1	5	4
6	4	4	3	7	6
3	1	1	0	4	3

Matrix Total

_____

(a)

6	4	4	3	7	6
5	3	3	2	6	5
8	6	6	5	9	8
4	2	2	1	5	4
6	4	4	3	7	6
3	1	1	0	4	3

4	2	2	5	3	6
6	4	4	7	5	8
3	1	1	4	2	5
7	5	5	8	6	9
4	2	2	5	3	6
5	3	3	6	4	7

Matrix Total

_____

(b)

4	2	2	5	3	6
6	4	4	7	5	8
3	1	1	4	2	5
7	5	5	8	6	9
4	2	2	5	3	6
5	3	3	6	4	7

6	4	8	4	7	5
3	1	5	1	4	2
7	5	9	5	8	6
4	2	6	2	5	3
5	3	7	3	6	4
2	0	4	0	3	1

Matrix Total

_____

(c)

6	4	8	4	7	5
3	1	5	1	4	2
7	5	9	5	8	6
4	2	6	2	5	3
5	3	7	3	6	4
2	0	4	0	3	1

7 × 7 and 8 × 8 matrices

Circle any number in a row and cross out the others in that row and column. Repeat this process until there is only one number remaining and circle this final number. Add up all the circled numbers. Choose different numbers in the next matrix and add the total of the circled numbers in each. What do you find?

10	6	13	27	8	19	24
9	5	12	26	7	18	23
16	12	19	33	14	25	30
22	18	25	39	20	31	36
13	9	16	30	11	22	27
18	14	21	35	16	27	32
24	20	27	41	22	33	38

Matrix Total _____ (a)

8	3	17	21	0	6	12	5
13	8	22	26	5	11	17	10
29	24	38	42	21	27	33	26
17	12	26	30	9	15	21	14
33	28	42	46	25	31	37	30
22	17	31	35	14	20	26	19
26	21	35	39	18	24	30	23
9	4	18	22	1	7	13	6

Matrix Total _____ (b)

9 × 9 and 10 × 10 matrices

Circle any number in a row and cross out the others in that row and column. Repeat this process until there is only one number remaining and circle this final number. Add up all the circled numbers. Choose different numbers in the next matrix and add the total of the circled numbers in each. What do you find?

29	15	20	34	32	17	23	22	27
19	5	10	24	22	7	13	12	17
16	2	7	21	19	4	10	9	14
41	27	32	46	44	29	35	34	39
26	12	17	31	29	14	20	19	24
31	17	22	36	34	19	25	24	29
40	26	31	45	43	28	34	33	38
46	32	37	51	49	34	40	39	44
37	23	28	42	40	25	31	30	35

Matrix Total _____ (a)

22	15	24	30	17	21	25	33	29	19
20	13	22	28	15	19	23	31	27	17
50	43	52	58	45	49	53	61	57	47
33	26	35	41	28	32	36	44	40	30
12	5	14	20	7	11	15	23	19	9
27	20	29	35	22	26	30	38	34	24
15	8	17	23	10	14	18	26	22	12
29	22	31	37	24	28	32	40	36	26
9	2	11	17	4	8	12	20	16	6
24	17	26	32	19	23	27	35	31	21

Matrix Total _____ (b)

3 × 3 decimal matrices

Circle any number in a row and cross out the others in that row and column. Repeat this process until there is only one number remaining and circle this final number. Add up all the circled numbers. Choose different numbers in the next matrix and add the total of the circled numbers in each. What do you find?

3.8	4.9	8.0
1.5	2.6	5.7
1.0	2.1	5.2

3.8	4.9	8.0
1.5	2.6	5.7
1.0	2.1	5.2

Matrix Total _____ (a)

1.3	3.0	4.6
3.4	5.1	6.7
5.3	7.0	8.6

1.3	3.0	4.6
3.4	5.1	6.7
5.3	7.0	8.6

Matrix Total _____ (b)

2.0	4.1	1.7
4.2	6.3	3.9
5.4	7.5	5.1

2.0	4.1	1.7
4.2	6.3	3.9
5.4	7.5	5.1

Matrix Total _____ (c)

2.5	0.3	1.6
5.6	3.4	4.7
7.2	5.0	6.3

2.5	0.3	1.6
5.6	3.4	4.7
7.2	5.0	6.3

Matrix Total _____ (d)

6.5	4.2	7.6
2.4	0.1	3.5
3.7	1.4	4.8

6.5	4.2	7.6
2.4	0.1	3.5
3.7	1.4	4.8

Matrix Total _____ (e)

7.6	7.0	4.9
4.4	3.8	1.7
5.0	4.4	2.3

7.6	7.0	4.9
4.4	3.8	1.7
5.0	4.4	2.3

Matrix Total _____ (f)

5.2	1.6	2.7
8.3	4.7	5.8
4.2	0.6	1.7

5.2	1.6	2.7
8.3	4.7	5.8
4.2	0.6	1.7

Matrix Total _____ (g)

6.2	2.7	1.2
7.4	8.9	2.4
9.0	5.5	4.0

6.2	2.7	1.2
7.4	8.9	2.4
9.0	5.5	4.0

Matrix Total _____ (h)

3 × 3 decimal matrices *(continued)*

Circle any number in a row and cross out the others in that row and column. Repeat this process until there is only one number remaining and circle this final number. Add up all the circled numbers. Choose different numbers in the next matrix and add the total of the circled numbers in each. What do you find?

6.0	7.6	6.4
3.7	5.3	4.1
5.3	6.9	5.7

6.0	7.6	6.4
3.7	5.3	4.1
5.3	6.9	5.7

Matrix Total _____ (a)

0.6	0.2	1.3
1.8	1.4	2.5
5.4	5.0	6.1

0.6	0.2	1.3
1.8	1.4	2.5
5.4	5.0	6.1

Matrix Total _____ (b)

5.9	3.7	4.4
7.4	5.2	5.9
9.7	7.5	8.2

5.9	3.7	4.4
7.4	5.2	5.9
9.7	7.5	8.2

Matrix Total _____ (c)

3.9	2.3	1.4
6.1	4.5	3.6
7.4	5.8	4.9

3.9	2.3	1.4
6.1	4.5	3.6
7.4	5.8	4.9

Matrix Total _____ (d)

2.5	3.6	1.8
3.7	4.8	3.0
1.2	2.3	0.5

2.5	3.6	1.8
3.7	4.8	3.0
1.2	2.3	0.5

Matrix Total _____ (e)

6.3	4.2	5.1
5.4	3.3	4.2
3.1	1.0	1.9

6.3	4.2	5.1
5.4	3.3	4.2
3.1	1.0	1.9

Matrix Total _____ (f)

3.6	2.2	1.7
4.9	3.5	3.0
5.8	4.4	3.9

3.6	2.2	1.7
4.9	3.5	3.0
5.8	4.4	3.9

Matrix Total _____ (g)

2.4	1.9	2.8
4.0	3.5	4.4
6.7	6.2	7.1

2.4	1.9	2.8
4.0	3.5	4.4
6.7	6.2	7.1

Matrix Total _____ (h)

3 × 3 fraction matrices

Circle any number in a row and cross out the others in that row and column. Repeat this process until there is only one number remaining and circle this final number. Add up all the circled numbers. Choose different numbers in the next matrix and add the total of the circled numbers in each. What do you find?

2	$3\frac{1}{2}$	1
$1\frac{1}{2}$	3	$\frac{1}{2}$
$4\frac{1}{2}$	6	$3\frac{1}{2}$

2	$3\frac{1}{2}$	1
$1\frac{1}{2}$	3	$\frac{1}{2}$
$4\frac{1}{2}$	6	$3\frac{1}{2}$

Matrix Total _____ (a)

$2\frac{1}{4}$	3	$3\frac{3}{4}$
$1\frac{1}{2}$	$2\frac{1}{4}$	3
2	$2\frac{3}{4}$	$3\frac{1}{2}$

$2\frac{1}{4}$	3	$3\frac{3}{4}$
$1\frac{1}{2}$	$2\frac{1}{4}$	3
2	$2\frac{3}{4}$	$3\frac{1}{2}$

Matrix Total _____ (b)

$2\frac{3}{4}$	$\frac{3}{4}$	2
$3\frac{1}{4}$	$1\frac{1}{4}$	$2\frac{1}{2}$
4	2	$3\frac{1}{4}$

$2\frac{3}{4}$	$\frac{3}{4}$	2
$3\frac{1}{4}$	$1\frac{1}{4}$	$2\frac{1}{2}$
4	2	$3\frac{1}{4}$

Matrix Total _____ (c)

$1\frac{3}{4}$	$2\frac{1}{4}$	$3\frac{1}{2}$
$2\frac{1}{2}$	3	$4\frac{1}{4}$
$3\frac{3}{4}$	$4\frac{1}{4}$	$5\frac{1}{2}$

$1\frac{3}{4}$	$2\frac{1}{4}$	$3\frac{1}{2}$
$2\frac{1}{2}$	3	$4\frac{1}{4}$
$3\frac{3}{4}$	$4\frac{1}{4}$	$5\frac{1}{2}$

Matrix Total _____ (d)

$1\frac{1}{6}$	$2\frac{2}{3}$	$1\frac{1}{3}$
$1\frac{1}{3}$	$2\frac{5}{6}$	$1\frac{1}{2}$
$1\frac{5}{6}$	$3\frac{1}{3}$	2

$1\frac{1}{6}$	$2\frac{2}{3}$	$1\frac{1}{3}$
$1\frac{1}{3}$	$2\frac{5}{6}$	$1\frac{1}{2}$
$1\frac{5}{6}$	$3\frac{1}{3}$	2

Matrix Total _____ (e)

$\frac{2}{3}$	3	$2\frac{1}{3}$
$1\frac{1}{6}$	$3\frac{1}{2}$	$2\frac{5}{6}$
$1\frac{1}{2}$	$3\frac{5}{6}$	$3\frac{1}{6}$

$\frac{2}{3}$	3	$2\frac{1}{3}$
$1\frac{1}{6}$	$3\frac{1}{2}$	$2\frac{5}{6}$
$1\frac{1}{2}$	$3\frac{5}{6}$	$3\frac{1}{6}$

Matrix Total _____ (f)

$2\frac{1}{3}$	$1\frac{2}{3}$	$3\frac{1}{2}$
$2\frac{2}{3}$	2	$3\frac{5}{6}$
$3\frac{1}{3}$	$2\frac{2}{3}$	$4\frac{1}{2}$

$2\frac{1}{3}$	$1\frac{2}{3}$	$3\frac{1}{2}$
$2\frac{2}{3}$	2	$3\frac{5}{6}$
$3\frac{1}{3}$	$2\frac{2}{3}$	$4\frac{1}{2}$

Matrix Total _____ (g)

$1\frac{1}{4}$	$2\frac{1}{6}$	1
$1\frac{7}{12}$	$2\frac{1}{2}$	$1\frac{1}{3}$
$1\frac{3}{4}$	$2\frac{2}{3}$	$1\frac{1}{2}$

$1\frac{1}{4}$	$2\frac{1}{6}$	1
$1\frac{7}{12}$	$2\frac{1}{2}$	$1\frac{1}{3}$
$1\frac{3}{4}$	$2\frac{2}{3}$	$1\frac{1}{2}$

Matrix Total _____ (h)

Circle any number in a row and cross out the others in that row and column. Repeat this process until there is only one number remaining and circle this final number. Add up all the circled numbers. Choose different numbers in the next matrix and add the total of the circled numbers in each. What do you find?

Matrix (a) - first:

$\frac{4}{5}$	$\frac{2}{5}$	$2\frac{1}{5}$
$1\frac{1}{5}$	$\frac{4}{5}$	$2\frac{3}{5}$
$1\frac{3}{5}$	$1\frac{1}{5}$	3

Matrix (a) - second:

$\frac{4}{5}$	$\frac{2}{5}$	$2\frac{1}{5}$
$1\frac{1}{5}$	$\frac{4}{5}$	$2\frac{3}{5}$
$1\frac{3}{5}$	$1\frac{1}{5}$	3

Matrix Total _____ (a)

Matrix (b) - first:

$2\frac{1}{10}$	0	$1\frac{1}{2}$
$2\frac{2}{5}$	$\frac{3}{10}$	$1\frac{4}{5}$
$2\frac{7}{10}$	$\frac{3}{5}$	$2\frac{1}{10}$

Matrix (b) - second:

$2\frac{1}{10}$	0	$1\frac{1}{2}$
$2\frac{2}{5}$	$\frac{3}{10}$	$1\frac{4}{5}$
$2\frac{7}{10}$	$\frac{3}{5}$	$2\frac{1}{10}$

Matrix Total _____ (b)

Matrix (c) - first:

2	$\frac{1}{16}$	$\frac{1}{8}$
$2\frac{1}{4}$	$\frac{5}{16}$	$\frac{3}{8}$
$2\frac{3}{4}$	$\frac{13}{16}$	$\frac{7}{8}$

Matrix (c) - second:

2	$\frac{1}{16}$	$\frac{1}{8}$
$2\frac{1}{4}$	$\frac{5}{16}$	$\frac{3}{8}$
$2\frac{3}{4}$	$\frac{13}{16}$	$\frac{7}{8}$

Matrix Total _____ (c)

Matrix (d) - first:

$2\frac{1}{3}$	$\frac{7}{12}$	$\frac{5}{6}$
$2\frac{2}{3}$	$\frac{11}{12}$	$1\frac{1}{6}$
$3\frac{1}{6}$	$1\frac{5}{12}$	$1\frac{2}{3}$

Matrix (d) - second:

$2\frac{1}{3}$	$\frac{7}{12}$	$\frac{5}{6}$
$2\frac{2}{3}$	$\frac{11}{12}$	$1\frac{1}{6}$
$3\frac{1}{6}$	$1\frac{5}{12}$	$1\frac{2}{3}$

Matrix Total _____ (d)

Matrix (e) - first:

2	$\frac{3}{4}$	$2\frac{5}{6}$
$2\frac{1}{2}$	$1\frac{1}{4}$	$3\frac{1}{3}$
3	$1\frac{3}{4}$	$3\frac{5}{6}$

Matrix (e) - second:

2	$\frac{3}{4}$	$2\frac{5}{6}$
$2\frac{1}{2}$	$1\frac{1}{4}$	$3\frac{1}{3}$
3	$1\frac{3}{4}$	$3\frac{5}{6}$

Matrix Total _____ (e)

Matrix (f) - first:

$1\frac{1}{3}$	$\frac{4}{15}$	3
$1\frac{2}{3}$	$\frac{3}{5}$	$3\frac{1}{3}$
$2\frac{1}{3}$	$1\frac{4}{15}$	4

Matrix (f) - second:

$1\frac{1}{3}$	$\frac{4}{15}$	3
$1\frac{2}{3}$	$\frac{3}{5}$	$3\frac{1}{3}$
$2\frac{1}{3}$	$1\frac{4}{15}$	4

Matrix Total _____ (f)

Matrix (g) - first:

3	$1\frac{1}{10}$	$1\frac{1}{2}$
$3\frac{1}{2}$	$1\frac{3}{5}$	2
4	$2\frac{1}{10}$	$2\frac{1}{2}$

Matrix (g) - second:

3	$1\frac{1}{10}$	$1\frac{1}{2}$
$3\frac{1}{2}$	$1\frac{3}{5}$	2
4	$2\frac{1}{10}$	$2\frac{1}{2}$

Matrix Total _____ (g)

Matrix (h) - first:

$1\frac{1}{2}$	$3\frac{3}{4}$	$\frac{3}{4}$
$2\frac{1}{4}$	$3\frac{1}{5}$	$1\frac{1}{2}$
3	$3\frac{19}{20}$	$2\frac{1}{4}$

Matrix (h) - second:

$1\frac{1}{2}$	$3\frac{3}{4}$	$\frac{3}{4}$
$2\frac{1}{4}$	$3\frac{1}{5}$	$1\frac{1}{2}$
3	$3\frac{19}{20}$	$2\frac{1}{4}$

Matrix Total _____ (h)

3 × 3 decimal/fraction matrices

Circle any number in a row and cross out the others in that row and column. Repeat this process until there is only one number remaining and circle this final number. Add up all the circled numbers. Choose different numbers in the next matrix and add the total of the circled numbers in each. What do you find?

1.5	3	0.75
$2\frac{1}{4}$	3.75	$1\frac{1}{2}$
2.5	4	1.75

1.5	3	0.75
$2\frac{1}{4}$	3.75	$1\frac{1}{2}$
2.5	4	1.75

Matrix Total _____ (a)

$3\frac{1}{2}$	2.5	4
2.25	$1\frac{1}{4}$	2.75
$2\frac{3}{4}$	1.75	$3\frac{1}{4}$

$3\frac{1}{2}$	2.5	4
2.25	$1\frac{1}{4}$	2.75
$2\frac{3}{4}$	1.75	$3\frac{1}{4}$

Matrix Total _____ (b)

0.9	0.3	1.7
1.8	$1\frac{1}{5}$	$2\frac{3}{5}$
$2\frac{1}{10}$	1.5	2.9

0.9	0.3	1.7
1.8	$1\frac{1}{5}$	$2\frac{3}{5}$
$2\frac{1}{10}$	1.5	2.9

Matrix Total _____ (c)

2.75	$1\frac{1}{4}$	0.6
$3\frac{1}{4}$	1.75	$1\frac{1}{10}$
3.75	$2\frac{1}{4}$	1.6

2.75	$1\frac{1}{4}$	0.6
$3\frac{1}{4}$	1.75	$1\frac{1}{10}$
3.75	$2\frac{1}{4}$	1.6

Matrix Total _____ (d)

$1\frac{1}{4}$	1.5	$2\frac{1}{2}$
0.5	$\frac{3}{4}$	1.75
$\frac{3}{4}$	1.0	2.0

$1\frac{1}{4}$	1.5	$2\frac{1}{2}$
0.5	$\frac{3}{4}$	1.75
$\frac{3}{4}$	1.0	2.0

Matrix Total _____ (e)

$2\frac{1}{10}$	$1\frac{1}{5}$	2.3
1.4	$\frac{1}{2}$	$1\frac{3}{5}$
$1\frac{7}{10}$	0.8	1.9

$2\frac{1}{10}$	$1\frac{1}{5}$	2.3
1.4	$\frac{1}{2}$	$1\frac{3}{5}$
$1\frac{7}{10}$	0.8	1.9

Matrix Total _____ (f)

0.7	$\frac{3}{10}$	$1\frac{1}{2}$
$\frac{9}{10}$	$\frac{1}{2}$	1.7
$1\frac{1}{5}$	0.8	2

0.7	$\frac{3}{10}$	$1\frac{1}{2}$
$\frac{9}{10}$	$\frac{1}{2}$	1.7
$1\frac{1}{5}$	0.8	2

Matrix Total _____ (g)

0.75	$2\frac{1}{2}$	0.5
$1\frac{1}{2}$	3.25	$1\frac{1}{4}$
2	$3\frac{3}{4}$	1.75

0.75	$2\frac{1}{2}$	0.5
$1\frac{1}{2}$	3.25	$1\frac{1}{4}$
2	$3\frac{3}{4}$	1.75

Matrix Total _____ (h)

3 × 3 decimal/fraction matrices *(continued)*

Circle any number in a row and cross out the others in that row and column. Repeat this process until there is only one number remaining and circle this final number. Add up all the circled numbers. Choose different numbers in the next matrix and add the total of the circled numbers in each. What do you find?

1.1	$\frac{9}{10}$	1.15
$\frac{7}{10}$	0.5	$\frac{3}{4}$
$\frac{1}{2}$	$\frac{3}{10}$	0.55

1.1	$\frac{9}{10}$	1.15
$\frac{7}{10}$	0.5	$\frac{3}{4}$
$\frac{1}{2}$	$\frac{3}{10}$	0.55

Matrix Total _____ (a)

$1\frac{1}{5}$	$2\frac{1}{2}$	$3\frac{2}{5}$
$\frac{3}{10}$	1.6	2.5
$1\frac{1}{2}$	$2\frac{4}{5}$	$3\frac{7}{10}$

$1\frac{1}{5}$	$2\frac{1}{2}$	$3\frac{2}{5}$
$\frac{3}{10}$	1.6	2.5
$1\frac{1}{2}$	$2\frac{4}{5}$	$3\frac{7}{10}$

Matrix Total _____ (b)

$\frac{1}{2}$	0.5	$1\frac{2}{5}$
0.8	$\frac{4}{5}$	1.7
$1\frac{2}{5}$	$1\frac{2}{5}$	$2\frac{3}{10}$

$\frac{1}{2}$	0.5	$1\frac{2}{5}$
0.8	$\frac{4}{5}$	1.7
$1\frac{2}{5}$	$1\frac{2}{5}$	$2\frac{3}{10}$

Matrix Total _____ (c)

$3\frac{4}{5}$	4.8	2.9
1.7	$2\frac{7}{10}$	$\frac{4}{5}$
$2\frac{1}{10}$	3.1	1.2

$3\frac{4}{5}$	4.8	2.9
1.7	$2\frac{7}{10}$	$\frac{4}{5}$
$2\frac{1}{10}$	3.1	1.2

Matrix Total _____ (d)

3.9	5.0	$3\frac{1}{2}$
2.3	3.4	1.9
$1\frac{4}{5}$	$2\frac{9}{10}$	$1\frac{2}{5}$

3.9	5.0	$3\frac{1}{2}$
2.3	3.4	1.9
$1\frac{4}{5}$	$2\frac{9}{10}$	$1\frac{2}{5}$

Matrix Total _____ (e)

$5\frac{4}{5}$	4.1	2.85
5.2	$3\frac{1}{2}$	$2\frac{1}{4}$
$3\frac{9}{10}$	2.2	0.95

$5\frac{4}{5}$	4.1	2.85
5.2	$3\frac{1}{2}$	$2\frac{1}{4}$
$3\frac{9}{10}$	2.2	0.95

Matrix Total _____ (f)

2.85	0.75	2.65
3.6	$1\frac{1}{2}$	$3\frac{2}{5}$
$4\frac{1}{5}$	2.1	4

2.85	0.75	2.65
3.6	$1\frac{1}{2}$	$3\frac{2}{5}$
$4\frac{1}{5}$	2.1	4

Matrix Total _____ (g)

4.75	3	$2\frac{1}{10}$
$5\frac{1}{4}$	3.5	$2\frac{3}{5}$
6.55	$4\frac{4}{5}$	$3\frac{9}{10}$

4.75	3	$2\frac{1}{10}$
$5\frac{1}{4}$	3.5	$2\frac{3}{5}$
6.55	$4\frac{4}{5}$	$3\frac{9}{10}$

Matrix Total _____ (h)

4 × 4 matrices – incomplete

Circle any number in a row and cross out the others in that row and column. Repeat this process until there is only one number remaining and circle this final number. Add up all the circled numbers. Choose different numbers in the next matrix and add the total of the circled numbers in each. What do you find?

(a)
			5
20	17	12	14
		28	
	26		

Matrix Total _____ (a)

(b)
		39	36
	15		
27	31	47	
		52	

Matrix Total _____ (b)

(c)
	7	10	14
6	2		
		16	
	11		

Matrix Total _____ (c)

(d)
	29	21	25
16	21		
21			
7			

Matrix Total _____ (d)

(e)
	37		
	31	27	36
12			24
5			

Matrix Total _____ (e)

(f)
12			
5	12	13	17
			15
			25

Matrix Total _____ (f)

4 × 4 matrices – incomplete *(continued)*

Circle any number in a row and cross out the others in that row and column. Repeat this process until there is only one number remaining and circle this final number. Add up all the circled numbers. Choose different numbers in the next matrix and add the total of the circled numbers in each. What do you find?

(a)

	9		
	14	26	30
8			21
11			

Matrix Total _____ (a)

(b)

	8	30	14
25	14		
		43	
	5		

Matrix Total _____ (b)

(c)

		25	39
	15		
20	7	14	
		7	

Matrix Total _____ (c)

(d)

11			
26	15	31	19
			28
			16

Matrix Total _____ (d)

(e)

			12
11	32	24	15
		31	
	25		

Matrix Total _____ (e)

(f)

11			
15	32	27	13
	38		
		21	

Matrix Total _____ (f)

4 × 4 matrices – incomplete *(continued)*

Circle any number in a row and cross out the others in that row and column. Repeat this process until there is only one number remaining and circle this final number. Add up all the circled numbers. Choose different numbers in the next matrix and add the total of the circled numbers in each. What do you find?

	10	6	1
25	21		
		26	
	27		

Matrix Total _____ (a)

			12
22	15	20	27
		23	
	9		

Matrix Total _____ (b)

		12	31
	13		
33	19	27	
		14	

Matrix Total _____ (c)

		3	9	19
14	9		
21			
29			

Matrix Total _____ (d)

	15		
	24	18	16
42			22
28			

Matrix Total _____ (e)

	14	15	9
16	29		
		38	
	22		

Matrix Total _____ (f)

5 × 5 matrices – incomplete

Circle any number in a row and cross out the others in that row and column. Repeat this process until there is only one number remaining and circle this final number. Add up all the circled numbers. Choose different numbers in the next matrix and add the total of the circled numbers in each. What do you find?

31		5	19	8
	9			3
		31		
	35			
	21			

Matrix Total _____ (a)

26	10		35	
		32		12
		52		
				38
	6			

Matrix Total _____ (b)

20		18	35	
		14		28
	28		34	
7				
		8		

Matrix Total _____ (c)

29	10		34	
45		34		61
		25		
19				
			27	

Matrix Total _____ (d)

Multiplication Matrices

These can be created in a similar way to Method 1 (page iii) when making matrices for addition except that all operations are now multiplication.

Example:–

Starting with a blank matrix complete a row with appropriate numbers

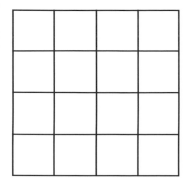 →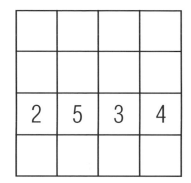

Multiply each number in the row by, for example 2

4	10	6	8
2	5	3	4

Multiply the original row by number eg 5

10	25	15	20
4	10	6	8
2	5	3	4

Finally multiply the original row by another number eg 3

10	25	15	20
4	10	6	8
2	5	3	4
6	15	9	12

To check the Magic Matrix Total multiply each set of diagonal numbers and they should be equal.

$$10 \times 10 \times 3 \times 12 = 3600$$
$$20 \times 6 \times 5 \times 6 = 3600$$

Multiplication Matrices *(continued)*

Use the same procedure for finding the Matrix Total as before, but this time **multiply** the chosen numbers.

10 × 8 × 5 × 9 = 3600

10	25	15	20
4	10	6	8
2	5	3	4
6	15	9	12

Now try these

10	14	6	6
15	21	9	9
5	7	3	3
20	28	12	12

Matrix Total = 7560

28	16	12	24
7	4	3	6
21	12	9	18
14	8	6	12

Matrix Total = 12096

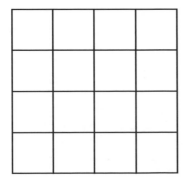

Matrix Total = ??????

Answers

Page

5 (a) 13	(b) 19	(c) 14	(d) 13	(e) 15	(f) 9	(g) 18	(h) 17
6 (a) 18	(b) 16	(c) 10	(d) 14	(e) 11	(f) 13	(g) 17	(h) 12
7 (a) 12	(b) 15	(c) 14	(d) 14	(e) 13	(f) 11	(g) 15	(h) 14
8 (a) 56	(b) 69	(c) 65	(d) 60	(e) 46	(f) 47	(g) 48	(h) 29
9 (a) 16	(b) 17	(c) 16	(d) 17				
10 (a) 21	(b) 20	(c) 20	(d) 16				
11 (a) 21	(b) 19	(c) 23	(d) 19				
12 (a) 18	(b) 22	(c) 20	(d) 19				
13 (a) 17	(b) 22	(c) 19	(d) 20				
14 (a) 18	(b) 18	(c) 19	(d) 20				
15 (a) 67	(b) 67	(c) 68	(d) 80				
16 (a) 96	(b) 81	(c) 89	(d) 89				
17 (a) 29	(b) 28	(c) 22					
18 (a) 26	(b) 23	(c) 25					
19 (a) 24	(b) 24	(c) 30					
20 (a) 27	(b) 27	(c) 20					
21 (a) 22	(b) 22	(c) 27					
22 (a) 32	(b) 27	(c) 29					
23 (a) 23	(b) 31	(c) 29					
24 (a) 24	(b) 30	(c) 26					
25 (a) 30	(b) 26	(c) 27					
26 (a) 28	(b) 26	(c) 30					
27 (a) 26	(b) 25	(c) 26					
28 (a) 26	(b) 27	(c) 25					
29 (a) 149	(b) 165						
30 (a) 243	(b) 256						
31 (a) 11.6	(b) 15	(c) 13.4	(d) 12.2	(e) 11.4	(f) 13.7	(g) 11.6	(h) 14.1
32 (a) 17	(b) 8.1	(c) 19.3	(d) 13.3	(e) 7.8	(f) 11.5	(g) 11	(h) 13
33 (a) $8\frac{1}{2}$	(b) 8	(c) $7\frac{1}{4}$	(d) $10\frac{1}{4}$	(e) 6	(f) $7\frac{1}{3}$	(g) $8\frac{5}{6}$	(h) $5\frac{1}{4}$
34 (a) $4\frac{3}{5}$	(b) $4\frac{1}{2}$	(c) $3\frac{3}{16}$	(d) $4\frac{11}{12}$	(e) $7\frac{1}{12}$	(f) $5\frac{14}{15}$	(g) $7\frac{1}{10}$	(h) $6\frac{19}{20}$
35 (a) 7	(b) 8	(c) 5	(d) 6.1	(e) 4	(f) 4.5	(g) 3.2	(h) 5.75
36 (a) 2.15	(b) 6.5	(c) 3.6	(d) 7.7	(e) 8.7	(f) 10.25	(g) 8.35	(h) 12.15
37 (a) 79	(b) 130	(c) 47	(d) 71	(e) 93	(f) 60		
38 (a) 67	(b) 87	(c) 81	(d) 82	(e) 79	(f) 83		
39 (a) 79	(b) 66	(c) 91	(d) 79	(e) 83	(f) 84		
40 (a) 112	(b) 148	(c) 106	(d) 142				

Answers (continued)

37 (a) 79

11	8	3	5
20	17	12	14
36	33	28	30
29	26	21	23

(b) 130

19	23	39	36
11	15	31	28
27	31	47	44
32	36	52	49

(c) 47

11	7	10	14
6	2	5	9
17	13	16	20
15	11	14	18

(d) 71

24	29	21	25
16	21	13	17
21	26	18	22
7	12	4	8

(e) 93

30	37	33	42
24	31	27	36
12	19	15	24
5	12	8	17

(f) 60

12	19	20	24
5	12	13	17
3	10	11	15
13	20	21	25

38 (a) 67

12	9	21	25
17	14	26	30
8	5	17	21
11	8	20	24

(b) 87

19	8	30	14
25	14	36	20
32	21	43	27
16	5	27	11

(c) 81

31	18	25	39
28	15	22	36
20	7	14	28
13	0	7	21

(d) 82

11	0	16	4
26	15	31	19
35	24	40	28
23	12	28	16

(e) 79

8	29	21	12
11	32	27	15
18	39	31	22
4	25	17	8

(f) 83

11	28	23	9
15	32	27	13
21	38	33	19
9	26	21	7